T

MW01714205

THE LAKE AT THE END OF THE WORLD

Loosely Adapted from an Inca Folk Tale

Script and Lyrics by David F. Eliet
Music by Nancy Rosenberg

Anchorage Press Plays, Inc.
ISBN: 978-0-87602-421-8

DEDICATED WITH LOVE TO
Mark, Kate, Rochelle, Mindy
and to
Colm and Carolyn

ORIGINAL PRODUCTION CREDIT

THE LAKE AT THE END OF THE WORLD was written for and originally produced by The Perishable Theatre in Providence, Rhode Island and toured throughout southern New England, July and August 1988.

Director: Larry Arrick
Musical Direction: Nancy Rosenberg
Choreography: April Shawhan

Original Cast:

Mindy Steinman	SUMAC/THE INCA'S SON
Mark Lerman	NARRATOR/THE INCA/SUMAC'S FATHER/GIANT CRAB/DRAGON
Rochelle Owen	COUNCILOR/SUMAC'S BROTHER/ GIANT CRAB/DRAGON
Kate Leach	DOCTOR 1/COURT DOCTOR/ FIRE SPIRIT/SUMAC'S MOTHER/ SPARROW

PRODUCTION NOTES

THE LAKE AT THE END OF THE WORLD was written for the children's touring company of The Perishable Theatre and was designed to be performed as simply as possible. Perishable performed under a variety of circumstances, often with no formal stage. In the style similar to middle-eastern street theatre, a large rug served as the stage, and props, costume pieces and musical instruments were placed around the edge of the rug. Onstage was on the rug, offstage was off the rug. All the actors served as the ensemble. When they were not featured in the scene, they would create the special effects, sing, or play non-speaking roles. Everything happened in view of the audience.

In this production of THE LAKE AT THE END OF THE WORLD, a hand puppet was used for the Sparrow. A gas mask, a long piece of fabric and one actor sitting on the shoulders of another made up the Dragon. The Giant Crab was created by two actors working in tandem, one on the back of the other facing in opposite directions with both knees and hands on the ground. The Llama was a child's bicycle, walked about by the actors, with a llama mask above the handlebars. The Magic Lake was created with a large piece of lightweight blue cloth, and fire with thin red strips of cloth.

Theatre groups should feel free to create as simple or elaborate a production as their resources allow.

Play Script Layout & Design: Randy Blevins, jrbdesign

CAST OF CHARACTERS

NARRATOR – Male
COUNCILOR – Male or Female
THE INCA'S SON – Male or Female
DOCTOR 1 – Male or Female
COURT DOCTOR – Male or Female
FIRE SPIRIT – Male or Female
SUMAC - Female
SUMAC'S BROTHER - Male
SUMAC'S FATHER - Male
SUMAC'S MOTHER – Female
LLAMA – Male or Female
SPARROW – Male or Female (music written for a woman)
GIANT CRAB – Male or Female
DRAGON – Male or Female
THE ENSEMBLE – The Actors

CASTING FOR FOUR ACTORS

SUMAC/THE INCA'S SON
NARRATOR/THE INCA/SUMAC'S FATHER/GIANT CRAB/DRAGON
COUNCILOR/SUMAC'S BROTHER/GIANT CRAB/DRAGON
DOCTOR 1/COURT DOCTOR/FIRE SPIRIT/SUMAC'S MOTHER/SPARROW

SETTING

Theatre groups should feel free to create as simple or elaborate a production as their resources allow. Suggested simple setting: A large rug serves as the stage. Props, costume pieces and musical instruments are placed around the edge of the rug. Onstage is on the rug, offstage is off the rug. Everything happens in view of the audience.

SONGS

(Shortened rehearsal titles in parenthesis)
MAGIC LAKE – Narrator, The Ensemble
PRAYER TO THE FIRE SPIRIT (Fire) – The Inca
I'M WALKING ACROSS THE ANDES (Walking Song) – Sumac's Brother
GREAT KING/INCA KING (See Me, Hear Me) – Sumac
I'M WALKING ACROSS THE ANDES Reprise (Sumac's Walking Song) – Sumac
I FEEL LIKE I'M FLYING (Flying) – Sparrow, Sumac
MAGIC LAKE Reprise – Narrator, The Ensemble

THE LAKE AT THE END OF THE WORLD

(Loosely Adapted from an Inca Folk Tale)
script and lyrics by David F. Eliet
music by Nancy Rosenberg

PROLOGUE

[SONG: THE MAGIC LAKE begins.] (The space is set for the performance and the actors enter.)

SONG: THE MAGIC LAKE

ENSEMBLE: *(Sings)*

Magic, Lake
Chic-a-chic, Lake.
Magic, Lake,
Chic-a-chic, Lake.

NARRATOR: *(Speaks)* We're going to tell you the story of the Magic Lake.

ENSEMBLE:
(Sings under narration)

Magic, Lake,
Chic-a-chic, Lake.
Magic, Lake,
Chic-a-chic, Lake.

King, King, King,
Inca King, King.

NARRATOR: *(Speaks)* The king needed water from the Magic Lake.

ENSEMBLE:
(Sings under narration)

King, King, King,
Inca King, King.

Magic, Lake,
Chic-a-chic, Lake.
Magic, Lake,
Chic-a-chic, Lake.
Boy, Boy, Boy
Naughty boy, Boy.

NARRATOR: *(Speaks)* The boy wanted gold from the king, for the water, he said, was the water from the Magic Lake.

ENSEMBLE:
(Sings under narration)

Boy, Boy, Boy
Naughty boy, Boy.

Magic, Lake,
Chic-a-chic, Lake.

Magic, Lake,
Chic-a-chic, Lake

ENSEMBLE-Women: *(Chant)*
Magic King–
Lake, Lake.
Lake, Lake, King–
Magic King–
Lake, Lake.
Lake, Lake, King.
(Repeat)

ENSEMBLE-Men: *(Chant)*
Chic-a-chic-a,
Chic-a-chic-a.
Chic-a-mah, chic-a-mah
Chic-a-chic-a-mah
Chic-a mah,
Chic-a-mah, Mah.
(Repeat)

ENSEMBLE: *(Sings)*

Dragon, terrible dragon.
Dragon, terrible dragon.
A terrible dragon.
Keeper of the water of the Magic—

NARRATOR: *(Speaks)* The Dragon was the keeper of the water that the king needed for his son—who was very sick in bed, very nearly dead. The boy tried to trick the king, whose son was ill, to get gold for water that wasn't the water from the Magic Lake.

ENSEMBLE:
(Sings under narration)

—Lake,
Chic-a-chic, Lake.
Magic, Lake,
Chic-a-chic, Lake.

Son, Son, Son,
Inca Son, Son
Son, Son, Son,
Inca Son, Son.

Magic, Lake,
Chic-a-chic, Lake.
Boy, Boy, Boy,
Awful boy, Boy.
Boy, Boy, Boy,
Awful boy, Boy.

Magic, Lake,
Chic-a-chic, Lake.
Magic, Lake,
Chic-a-chic, Lake.

ENSEMBLE-Women: *(Chant)*
Magic King–
Lake, Lake.
Lake, Lake, King–
Magic King–
Lake, Lake.
Lake, Lake, King.
(Repeat)

ENSEMBLE-Men: *(Chant)*
Chic-a-chic-a,
Chic-a-chic-a.
Chic-a-mah, Chic-a-mah
Chic-a-chic-a-mah
Chic-a mah,
Chic-a-mah, Mah.
(Repeat)

ENSEMBLE: *(Sings)*
Sumac was the girl
Who found the lake and
Beat the dragon
Saving the son of the Inca king
All with the water
Of the Magic, Lake
Chic-a-chic, Lake.

Magic, Lake,
Chic-a-chic, Lake.

NARRATOR: *(Speaks)* So, Sumac was the little girl who found the Magic Lake.

ENSEMBLE:
(Sings under narration)
Magic, Lake
Chic-a-chic, Lake.
Magic, Lake
Chic-a-chic, Lake.
Magic Lake, Magic Lake
Magic Lake!

NARRATOR: *(Speaks)* We're going to tell you the story of the Magic Lake.
(End of song; transformation into the first scene)

SCENE ONE

THE INCA: *(To the audience)* Once, long ago, before Christopher Columbus came to the western world, there was a mighty king, The Inca, who ruled over a great and powerful people known as the Incas. He was The Inca among Incas.

COUNCILOR: He was richer than any man in the world.

THE INCA: *(Counting his gold)* Thirty-three billion, one hundred and forty million, eight hundred fifty-five thousand, seven hundred twenty-five dollars, and sixteen cents.

COUNCILOR: He had everything a king could want - stone

palaces, beautiful clothing, lots of food, and a million other things. In fact, there was only one thing in the whole world The Inca didn't have, and that was happiness. And the reason he wasn't happy—

THE INCA: –was because of my son. Councilor!

COUNCILOR: Yes, Your Majesty?

THE INCA: Bring me my son.

COUNCILOR: At once, Your Majesty. *(Exits)*

THE INCA: My son, my only child, is ill. In fact, he is dying. I am an old man. I cannot live forever. And unless someone can do something to cure my son, he will not live to be king after me. Then my people will have no leader, our enemies will attack us, and the kingdom of the Incas will vanish. *(Councilor reenters with The Inca's Son.)* How is my son today? Is he any better?

COUNCILOR: I'm afraid not, Your Majesty.

THE INCA: Then bring in the doctors.

COUNCILOR: *(To the audience)* So, every day, doctors were brought from all over the kingdom to try and cure the King's son. *(Claps his hands)*

DOCTOR 1: *(Enters and bows to The Inca)* Your Majesty.

THE INCA: Have you examined my son?

DOCTOR 1: I have.

THE INCA: What do you think is wrong with him?

DOCTOR 1: Your son suffers from a complex tubular linguosis of the upper, lower thorax.

THE INCA: And is there any hope that he can be cured?

DOCTOR 1: Fortunately for you, I have arrived just in time. However, I must warn you that this cure is very expensive—very expensive.

THE INCA: I don't care what it costs, as long as you make my son better.

DOCTOR 1: Very well.
(Doctor 1 takes a bunch of vials from a bag and mixes them together making an ugly looking mixture. He holds the boy's nose

and pours liquid down his throat. There is a pause. Suddenly the king's son starts to scream, clutches his throat, his eyes bug out, and he runs in circles around the stage.)

THE INCA: What have you done? What's wrong with my son?

DOCTOR 1: Wrong? There's nothing wrong. He's cured. Why just a few moments ago he could hardly walk, and now he's running around like any healthy child.
(The Inca's Son stops dead in his tracks, places his hands to his head, lets out one final scream and falls over.)

THE INCA: Is he dead?

DOCTOR 1: Of course not. He's just resting after all that exercise.

THE INCA: Councilor?

COUNCILOR: *(Bending over and feeling the boy's pulse)* His pulse is very weak, and he is burning up with fever.
(He helps The Inca's Son offstage.)

THE INCA: You haven't made my son better, you have made him worse.

DOCTOR 1: That's not true. Wait a few minutes and you'll see. The potion I gave him is very magical. It can cure anything.

THE INCA: Anything?

DOCTOR 1: Oh, yes. I promise.

THE INCA: Then let it cure this.
(Grabs the mixture from Doctor 1 and pours it down Doctor 1's throat)

DOCTOR 1: What are you doing? No! Wait! Stop! Help!
(Doctor 1 gags and runs screaming from the stage.)

COUNCILOR: *(To the audience as he reenters)* Finally, after days and weeks and months of trying everything possible, it was clear that there was no one who could save the life of the King's son.

THE INCA: You're worthless. All of you are absolutely, positively, without the slightest, possible doubt, worthless.

COUNCILOR: But Your Majesty—

THE INCA: Worthless!

COUNCILOR: But everything that can be done has been done.

THE INCA: Then think of something new.

COUNCILOR: There isn't anything else.

THE INCA: There has to be. There just has to be. *(He walks in a circle, thinking, then stops.)* I know. I will pray to the Fire Spirit. I will offer my life for the life of my son. Prepare the ceremony.

[SONG: PRAYER TO THE FIRE SPIRIT (Fire) begins.]

(The Inca and the space are prepared for the ceremony.)

SONG: PRAYER TO THE FIRE SPIRIT (Fire)
THE INCA:
(Kneeling before the fire, chants)

Fire! Fire!
Giver of heat
Giver of light
I call to you
O mighty one
Who lives within the
Fire, fire, fire
God of the heat
God of the light
On bended knees
I pray to you
Show me what to do
Show me how to save my son
And I will give my life to
Fire, fire.
Giver of heat
Giver of life
Show me
Show me
Show me.

(There are loud sounds and thunder. The flames of the fire shoot up. The Fire Spirit emerges. Music continues under the scene.)

FIRE SPIRIT: If your son is to live, he must drink of the water of the lake at the end of the world. Only the water from that lake can heal him. And only in that way, and in that way only, can his life be saved.

THE INCA: But how do I find the lake?

FIRE SPIRIT: Only someone who is pure at heart can go there and return.

THE INCA: But who?

FIRE SPIRIT: *(Holding out a golden bottle)* Take this golden flask. It will show you what is false and what is true.

THE INCA: What do you mean, "what is false and what is true?"

FIRE SPIRIT: *(Starting to die down)* Remember, you have promised me your life if your son's is saved. *(Exits)*

THE INCA: *(Taking the flask and holding it up to the audience)* Then let it be known throughout all my lands that whomever brings me the water from the Magic Lake shall be rewarded with riches beyond his wildest dreams. *(Exits. Music ends.)*

SCENE TWO

SUMAC'S BROTHER: *(Stepping onto the stage)* Now, almost everyone in the land of the Incas went looking for the Magic Lake: soldiers, noblemen, rich people and poor, especially poor people. Poor people like me.

SUMAC'S FATHER: *(Entering)* Son, have you weeded the fields yet?

SUMAC'S MOTHER: *(Entering)* Son, have you taken out the garbage yet?

SUMAC'S BROTHER: Except me. They won't let me go. Parents. They never understand.

SUMAC'S FATHER: It's too dangerous. There are jaguars and other wild animals.

SUMAC'S BROTHER: Dad, I'm not a baby.

SUMAC'S MOTHER: But who's going to cook your meals, wash your clothes, tell you to take a bath?

SUMAC'S BROTHER: Mom.

SUMAC'S FATHER: Besides, I need you here to help with the harvest.

SUMAC'S BROTHER: But think of the reward if I'm successful.

Think of all that gold.

SUMAC'S MOTHER/FATHER: Gold?

SUMAC'S BROTHER: Lots of gold. We could have a big house—

SUMAC'S MOTHER: Lots to eat and drink—

SUMAC'S FATHER: Beautiful clothes and lots of—

THE THREE OF THEM: GOLD!

SUMAC'S MOTHER: Perhaps the boy is right.

SUMAC'S FATHER: The harvest is still a long ways off, and Sumac can help me until then.

SUMAC: *(Entering)* Not me. I'm going too.

SUMAC'S BROTHER: You can't go. You're a girl.

SUMAC: So?

SUMAC'S BROTHER: So, girls can't go on adventures. Only boys can.

SUMAC: That's not true.

SUMAC'S BROTHER: It is.

SUMAC: Is not.
(They continue with "is", "isn't" until interrupted by Sumac's Father.)

SUMAC'S FATHER: Sumac! That's enough out of you.

SUMAC: Please, Father.

SUMAC'S FATHER: Your brother is right. Good luck, my son.
(Sumac's Father and Mother exit. Sumac's Mother kisses her son as she leaves.)

SUMAC'S BROTHER: *(To the audience)* So, Sumac's brother got ready to set off to find the Magic Lake at the end of the world. He took some food his mother had given him, and a llama to carry his things. *(To Sumac as he starts to leave)* Good-bye Sumac. *(She pays no attention.)* I said good-bye, Sumac. *(Slight pause)* Aren't you going to say good-bye to me?

SUMAC: Why? You won't get very far. You'll probably be back as soon as it gets dark out.

SUMAC'S BROTHER: Will not.

SUMAC: Will. You'll be afraid.

SUMAC'S BROTHER: Of what?

SUMAC: Bandits, wild animals, monsters, ghosts.

SUMAC'S BROTHER: I'm not afraid of anything.

SUMAC: Hah!

SUMAC'S BROTHER: You'd better take that back.

SUMAC: I won't.

SUMAC'S BROTHER: Take it back, or I won't give you any of the gold I'll get when I find the Magic Lake.

SUMAC: *(Exiting)* See you tonight.

SUMAC'S BROTHER: *(Calling after her)* I warned you. *(To audience)* Afraid. I'm not afraid.

SCENE THREE

SUMAC'S BROTHER: What's there to be afraid of? Nothing. I'm big and strong. *[SONG: I'M WALKING ACROSS THE ANDES begins.]* Nothing would dare attack me. And if it did, I'd take care of it all right.

SONG: I'M WALKING ACROSS THE ANDES (Walking Song)
SUMAC'S BROTHER: *(Sings)*

Sun above me
The sky is clear
Road before me
I have no fear
I'm walking
Across the Andes
Back bone of sweet
Mother Earth
I'm walking, walking on.

(Speaks to the audience) Bandits? Why if some old bandit attacked me, I'd grab his knife right out of his hand, and then I'd give him a left and then a right, and a right and a left. I'd throw him to his knees and shove him off the mountain. That's what I'd do to a bandit.

(Sings)

Trees beside me
The river's near
Birds are singing
The song is clear
I'm searching
Across the Andes
For the riches
Of the earth.
I'm searching, searching on.

Gold before me
My goal is clear
I know that
Fame is calling
And wealth is near
Yes I am hunting
For a lake that lies
At the end of
Mother Earth

(Speaks as music continues) Ghosts and monsters. They don't frighten me.

(Sings)

Sun above me
The gold is near.
Road before me
I have no fear.
I will find this lake
That's hidden
At the end of
Mother Earth.
I'm walking, walking,
Walking, walking on.

(Speaks as the music fades) Now, as to wild animals, I'm meaner and wilder than any wild animal. If one of them came near me, I'd—

(A jaguar roars, voiced by one of the Ensemble.)

SUMAC'S BROTHER: I'd—
(Jaguar roars again.)
What was that?

ENSEMBLE Member (who voiced the jaguar): A jaguar!

SUMAC'S BROTHER: A JAGUAR! *(He runs around, terrified.)* Help! Help! Mommy! Mommy! Save me! *(He ends up hiding behind the llama.)* It's a good thing I've got this llama. A jaguar would rather eat a llama than a person any day. *(He waits a* *second then peers out from behind the llama.)* Is he gone? *(He comes out slowly and looks around.)* Hello? Anyone out there? Hello? *(When it is clear the jaguar is gone, he slowly gets brave again.)* I guess that stupid jaguar knows who's boss. Lucky for him he didn't attack me, or he would've gotten hurt real bad. *(Sparrow enters behind him.)* Why I'd have—

SPARROW: Hello.

SUMAC'S BROTHER: YEEEOW!
(He dives behind the llama again.)

SPARROW: I'm sorry. I didn't mean to scare you.

SUMAC'S BROTHER: *(To audience)* It's just a talking sparrow. Wait a minute, sparrows can't talk.

SPARROW: Who says?

SUMAC'S BROTHER: That's just the—

SPARROW: Then you must be hearing things.

SUMAC'S BROTHER: I must be.

SPARROW: Good. I'm glad that's settled. Now what are you doing hiding behind that llama?

SUMAC'S BROTHER: *(To Sparrow as he comes out of hiding)* I wasn't hiding. And you didn't scare me.

SPARROW: Oh.

SUMAC'S BROTHER: *(Taking out some food)* I was just getting my lunch. I'm hungry. I've been looking for that stupid Magic Lake for almost an hour, and I still haven't found it. *(Sits down and begins to eat)*

SPARROW: Please, kind sir, could you possibly spare a poor, hungry sparrow a wee bite to eat? I don't need much, just a few crumbs from your tortilla, or a couple of grains of corn.

SUMAC'S BROTHER: No way.

SPARROW: Please.

SUMAC'S BROTHER: I said, "No."

SPARROW: You should have more respect for the needs of others.

SUMAC'S BROTHER: I have respect for the needs of my stomach. *(He eats and Sparrow inches closer.)* Get away from me. *(Waving at Sparrow until it hops off; pause)*

SPARROW: You'll never find the Magic Lake, if you keep stopping to eat every five minutes.

SUMAC'S BROTHER: I'll find it all right.

SPARROW: Besides, you're going in the wrong direction.

SUMAC'S BROTHER: Then tell me where it is.

SPARROW: Give me something to eat.

SUMAC'S BROTHER: Oh, no. I'm not going to be fooled that easily. You have to tell me first.

SPARROW: No. First the food and then the lake. You have to trust me.

SUMAC'S BROTHER: Trust you? I'm not going to trust you.

SPARROW: This is your last chance.

SUMAC'S BROTHER: You probably don't even know where the lake is anyhow.

SPARROW: I do. But getting there is very dangerous.

SUMAC'S BROTHER: I'm not afraid.

SPARROW: And it's far away.

SUMAC'S BROTHER: How far is far?

SPARROW: High over the mountains where the earth touches the sky.

SUMAC'S BROTHER: That far.

SPARROW: And farther.

SUMAC'S BROTHER: *(Discouraged)* I'll never get there. And even if I do, the king's son will probably already be dead by the time I get back, and I won't get any reward.

SPARROW: Well, there is another lake just up ahead.

SUMAC'S BROTHER: So?

SPARROW: So—Lake.

SUMAC'S BROTHER: Lake.

SPARROW: Water.

SUMAC'S BROTHER: Water.

SPARROW: Lake and water.

SUMAC'S BROTHER: Lake and water. *(Leaping to his feet as he gets it)* Lake and water. I could fill my water jug up at that lake, and be back at the palace before dark. After all, water is just water. Nobody can tell where it came from.

SPARROW: And the king's son?

SUMAC'S BROTHER: What about him?

SPARROW: He could die from the wrong water.

SUMAC'S BROTHER: He's going to die anyway, so what does it matter? *(He starts to exit.)*

SPARROW: Hey, what about my food?

SUMAC'S BROTHER: What about it?

SPARROW: But you said—

SUMAC'S BROTHER: So long, Bird Brain. *(He exits.)*

ACTOR WHO PLAYED SPARROW: And so, Sumac's brother filled his jug with water from a lake that wasn't the lake, and set off to the palace of the king.
(ACTOR exits as The Inca and Sumac's Brother enter.)

SCENE FOUR

THE INCA: You will be richly rewarded for bringing me the water from the Magic Lake.

SUMAC'S BROTHER: I was counting on that.

THE INCA: Name whatever you want, and it will be yours.

SUMAC'S BROTHER: How about a small mountain of gold?

THE INCA: *(Reaching for the water jug)* Done.

SUMAC'S BROTHER: *(Pulling the jug away)* With a river of silver flowing down the side—for a bit of color.

THE INCA: *(Pulling jug towards himself)* Done.

SUMAC'S BROTHER: *(Pulling jug back)* And maybe a bucket of emeralds and diamonds—

THE INCA: *(Pulling jug towards himself)* Done. Done.

SUMAC'S BROTHER: *(Pulling jug back)* And some opals and rubies and sapphires—

THE INCA: *(Pulling jug towards himself)* Done. Done. *(Wrestling jug from Sumac's Brother)* And done! *(Calling offstage)* Now bring me my son.

(The Court Doctor enters helping The Inca's Son.)

THE INCA: This is a joyous day, my son, for before you is water from the Magic Lake. The Fire Spirit has promised me that this water will cure you. *(Lifting the jug)* Here, drink. *(The Inca's Son can barely hold out his hands, let alone take the jug.)* Doctor, help him.

(The Court Doctor takes the jug and tips it to The Inca's Son's mouth. The Inca's Son takes a sip and falls over.)

THE INCA: What's this?

COURT DOCTOR: *(Helping The Inca's Son to his feet)* Taking that drink of water has exhausted him.

THE INCA: But this cannot be. The water is supposed to cure him.

COURT DOCTOR: Perhaps he wasn't supposed to drink the water. After all, the Fire Spirit never said what we should do with it. Perhaps we should try something else.

THE INCA: Like what?

COURT DOCTOR: Like sprinkling it on him.

THE INCA: Try it. *(The Court Doctor does so. The Inca's Son starts to sneeze and tremble.)* What's wrong now?

COURT DOCTOR: He seems to have caught a chill from the water.

(The Inca's Son's sneezing carries him offstage.)

COURT DOCTOR: I don't understand. The Fire Spirit promised the water from the Magic Lake would cure him. He even gave you a golden flask as a sign that this was so.

THE INCA: That's it! The golden flask. Fetch me the golden flask. He has to drink the water from the golden flask. Then he'll be cured.
(The Court Doctor produces the golden flask.)

THE INCA: (*Handing the Court Doctor the water jug)* Here. Pour in the water.
(The Court Doctor tries to pour the water into the golden flask. There is an explosion and flames shoot from the flask. This may simply be a sound effect with reactions from the actors. The Inca and the Court Doctor jump back.)

COURT DOCTOR: It's like the Fire Spirit doesn't want this water in that flask.

THE INCA: I've got it. It's like the Fire Spirit doesn't want that water in this flask.

COURT DOCTOR: I don't understand.

THE INCA: By not letting the water in, the flask is showing me that this is not the true water from the Magic Lake, and that this boy is false. He is not pure at heart. He is a liar and a cheat.

SUMAC'S BROTHER: I'm not.

THE INCA: That is just ordinary water from an ordinary lake.

SUMAC'S BROTHER: It isn't.

THE INCA: Then prove it.

SUMAC'S BROTHER: How?

THE INCA: Take the flask and pour all the water in at once.

SUMAC'S BROTHER: And get burned up?

THE INCA: If this is the water from the Magic Lake, then you are pure at heart, and the fire will not harm you. Now pour the water.

SUMAC'S BROTHER: No. No.

THE INCA: DO IT!

SUMAC'S BROTHER: *(Trying to escape, he is stopped by the Court Doctor.)* No. Please.

THE INCA: NOW!

SUMAC'S BROTHER: I can't. It's not the water from the Magic Lake. You were right, I was lying.

THE INCA: And for that you must be severely punished.

SUMAC'S BROTHER: Please spare me, Your Majesty. I did it for my family. I wasn't going to keep any of the reward for myself. Honest.

THE INCA: You are a greedy, little liar. And you will be burned to death for having offended the Fire Spirit.

SUMAC'S BROTHER: No. No. I'm sorry. Really I am.

THE INCA: Too late.

(Sumac rushes in.)

COURT DOCTOR: Wait. You can't come in here.
(She throws herself at The Inca's feet.)

SUMAC: Please, Your Majesty, spare my brother, and I will bring you the water from the Magic Lake.

THE INCA: What is this? Is this a girl? Have you let a girl into my presence?

COURT DOCTOR: I tried to stop her, but she got away.

SUMAC: My name is Sumac.

COURT DOCTOR: Her name is Sumac.

THE INCA: Well, what is she doing here?

SUMAC: My parents sent me when they heard my brother had found the Magic Lake.

COURT DOCTOR: Her parents told her to come.

SUMAC: I was supposed to help him carry home the reward.

COURT DOCTOR: She was supposed to help him carry home the loot.

THE INCA: Well, now she can carry home his ashes.

SUMAC: Please, give me a chance.

COURT DOCTOR: She says give her a chance.

THE INCA: Never! Light the fire!

SUMAC: NO! YOU MUSTN'T!

COURT DOCTOR: *(Getting carried away)* No. You mustn't.

THE INCA: What?

COURT DOCTOR: *(Composing himself)* The girl says you mustn't.

THE INCA: Yes. She is right.

COURT DOCTOR: She is?

THE INCA: Burning him right away is much too kind. First he must be thrown into my deepest, darkest, dirtiest dungeon, with only the water he brought me to live on.

SUMAC: No, please.

THE INCA: And then, when that is all gone, he will be burned to death.

SUMAC: Tortured and then burned. But why?

THE INCA: Because he has offended the Fire Spirit. The Inca has spoken!

SONG: GREAT KING/INCA KING (See Me, Hear Me)
SUMAC: *(Sings)*

Great king
Inca king
Please see me,
Hear me.
You know my brother's
Locked away
Locked in cruel darkness
Of a dungeon
Out of sight
Out of light of day

Far beneath the
Earth, rock and stone
You know he lies in fear
Truly, surely
He will perish
Unless you
See me
Hear me

THE INCA: *(Speaking over "Hear me...")* Your brother will die. There is nothing you can do to save him.

SUMAC: *(Sings)*

Your only son lays dying
He lays in the darkness
Of a bedroom
Far above the
Trees and stones
Out of sight
Out of light of day
Great King, Inca King
Please look now
See now
For like my brother dear
Truly, surely
He will perish
Unless you will see me
Oh please won't you see me
Hear me

SUMAC: *(Speaks as music ends)* I will bring you the water from the Magic Lake, if only you will spare the life of my brother.

THE INCA: But if you fail?

SUMAC: It will be because I am dead.

THE INCA: What do you think, Doctor?

COURT DOCTOR: The mightiest heroes in the land have been unable to find the lake. But the Fire Spirit did say the lake could only be found by someone who is pure at heart, so maybe she can succeed where the others have failed. Besides if she doesn't succeed, you can still barbecue this miserable wretch.

THE INCA: All right. But if you fail, your brother will die.

SUMAC: Thank you, Your Majesty. Thank you.
(The Inca, Court Doctor and Sumac's Brother exit.)

SCENE FIVE

SUMAC: *(To audience)* So Sumac set off to find the Magic Lake. And like her brother before her, she had a llama along to help carry her things.

SONG: I'M WALKING ACROSS THE ANDES (REPRISE)
(Sumac's Walking Song)
SUMAC: *(Sings)*

Sun above me
The sky is clear
Road before me
The path is near
I'm walking for the water
That will save my brother dear
I'm searching, searching on.

(A jaguar roars, voiced by one of the Ensemble.)

SUMAC: *(Speaks)* What was that? *(Jaguar roars again. Music ends.)* A jaguar. My llama. My llama's in danger. *(Taking her things off the llama she guides its exit)* Quick. Run home. You'll be safe there.

(The llama exits, assisted by one of the Ensemble.)

SPARROW: *(Entering)* Well, that was certainly a dumb thing to do.

SUMAC: Who said that?

SPARROW: Who do you think?

SUMAC: A talking sparrow?

SPARROW: At your service.

SUMAC: But sparrows can't talk.

SPARROW: Please, I've already been through this with your dumb brother.

SUMAC: You've met my brother?

SPARROW: I'll say. And what a creep he was.

SUMAC: You shouldn't talk about my brother like that.

SPARROW: All right, we'll talk about your llama instead.

SUMAC: What about it?

SPARROW: Well, what are you going to do now? How are you going to carry all your things?

SUMAC: I—

SPARROW: And how are you going to stay warm at night without the llama to sleep next to?

SUMAC: Well—

SPARROW: And what about the jaguar? With no llama to eat, he'll have to settle for girl. What about that, huh?

SUMAC: I couldn't keep the llama with me, just so the jaguar wouldn't eat me, could I?

SPARROW: Why not?

SUMAC: Because it's not his fault my brother got caught trying to cheat The Inca.

SPARROW: You certainly are a softy, aren't you? Give me something to eat.

SUMAC: What?

SPARROW: I said, "Give me something to eat."

SUMAC: You're very bossy. You must really be hungry.

SPARROW: Maybe I am and maybe I'm not.

SUMAC: I don't have very much food with me, and it has to last a long time, but I'll give you what I can.
(Hands Sparrow some food)

SPARROW: Thank you.

SUMAC: You're welcome.

SPARROW: *(Starting to eat)* So, you're looking for the lake at the end of the world.

SUMAC: Yes.

SPARROW: Which way are you going to go?

SUMAC: *(Pointing in a direction)* That way.

SPARROW: It's not that way.

SUMAC: *(Pointing in another direction)* Then I'll go that way.

SPARROW: It's not that way either.

SUMAC: *(Pointing in a third direction)* Over there?

SPARROW: Nope.

SUMAC: Then that leaves... *(Points)*

SPARROW: Wrong again.

SUMAC: It has to be in one of those directions.

SPARROW: If it was an ordinary lake, it would. But this is the lake at the end of the world—the Magic Lake. And to that lake no man—I mean girl—can ever go unless...

SUMAC: Unless?

SPARROW: Unless, she has help.

SUMAC: Can you help me?

SPARROW: Maybe I can, and maybe I can't.

SUMAC: Please, please, please help me.

SPARROW: First you have to promise me something.

SUMAC: All right.

SPARROW: How can you promise when you don't even know what it is?

SUMAC: It doesn't matter. I'll promise. I trust you.

SPARROW: All right then. After you've found the lake and taken the water to the king, he will be so happy that he will forget all about the awful thing your brother did, and he will offer you anything you want as a reward. But if I am to help you, you must promise not to ask for anything for yourself.

SUMAC: Okay.

SPARROW: Not one jewel, or fancy clothes, or any money, or even a new toy. Nothing.

SUMAC: I promise.

SPARROW: You do?

SUMAC: Yes.

SPARROW: Now why would you make a stupid promise like that?

SUMAC: It's easy. All I really want to do is save my brother.

SPARROW: All right. *(Pulling a feather out)* Now this is a magic feather. It will take you anywhere you want to go. It will protect you from danger. And if there is anything you need, just ask, and it will come to you.

SUMAC: Wow.

SPARROW: Never, never let go of it for any reason.

SUMAC: I won't.

SPARROW: Good. Now be on your way. *(Sparrow starts to exit.)*

SUMAC: Oh, wait. *[SONG: I FEEL LIKE I'M FLYING (Flying) begins]* Wait! I don't know how it works.

SPARROW: *(Stopping)* Oh, right. Sorry.

SONG: I FEEL LIKE I'M FLYING (Flying)

SPARROW: *(Sings)*

Eyes shut
Feet together
Feather in your hand
Eyes shut
Knees bent
Feather in your hand
Take her
Take her
Take her to the magic land
Eyes shut

SUMAC: *(Sings)* Eyes shut

SPARROW: *(Sings)* Feet together

SUMAC: *(Sings)* Feet together, feather

SPARROW/SUMAC: *(Sing)* Feather in your/my hand.

SPARROW: *(Sings)* Eyes shut

SUMAC: *(Sings)* Eyes shut

SPARROW: *(Sings)* Knees bent

SUMAC: *(Sings)* Knees are bent, a feather

SPARROW/SUMAC: *(Sing)*

Feather in your/my hand
Take her/me
Take her/me
Take her/me
To the magic land!

SUMAC: *(Sings)*

I feel like I am flying
The wind is in my hair
The sun is in my face
And I've got a feather
Held tightly in my hand.
What could I see
If I opened up my eyes?
Tree tops, mountains,
Valleys and rivers,
A dove on my left hand,
An eagle on my right.
Does the world look the same
From such a mighty height?

SPARROW: *(Sings)* Eyes shut, Feet together

SUMAC: *(Sings)* Feet together, feather

SPARROW/SUMAC: *(Sing)* Feather in your/my hand

SPARROW: *(Sings)* Eyes shut

SUMAC: *(Sings)* Eyes shut

SPARROW: *(Sings)* Knees bent

SUMAC: *(Sings)* Knees are bent, a feather

SPARROW/SUMAC: *(Sing)*

Feather in your/my hand.
Take her/me
Take her/me
Take her/me
To the magic land!

SCENE SIX

(The music ends and Sparrow exits.)

SUMAC: *(Opening her eyes, she is at the Magic Lake.)* So this is it. The feather really is magic. Now all I have to do is get the water and be on my way. *(Looks around her)* Oh no, I left everything behind. I didn't bring a jug to put the water in. How will I carry it? *(Stops)* The feather. What did the sparrow say? If you need anything... All right. Here I go. *(She shuts her eyes.)* Magic feather, I need something to hold the water. *(The golden flask is flown in and lands at her feet. She opens her eyes.)* Wow! That certainly isn't my water jug. *(She approaches the water. There is a sudden boiling up of the water. Sumac drops the flask.)* Help! Help! A storm!

(Giant Crab appears out of the water.)

SUMAC: Oh, no. A giant crab!

GIANT CRAB: *(Opening and shutting its claws)* Snap. Snap. *(Pointing to the flask that is at its feet)* You forgot something.

SUMAC: *(Running to get the flask)* I've got to get the golden flask.

GIANT CRAB: *(Grabbing her)* Who dares to approach the Magic Lake?

SUMAC: It's just me, Sumac.

GIANT CRAB: Ah, a tender little morsel. I'll dine well today. Girl Salad.

SUMAC: No. You mustn't. *(She holds her hands up in front of her and in so doing places the feather in front of Giant Crab's eyes.)*

GIANT CRAB: What's that?

SUMAC: Nothing. Just a feather the sparrow gave me.

GIANT CRAB: *(Starting to go limp)* Did you say a feather?

SUMAC: Yes.

GIANT CRAB: From a sparrow?

SUMAC: *(Breaking free)* Yes.

GIANT CRAB: To protect you from a giant crab?

SUMAC: *(Starting to back Giant Crab up)* Yes.

GIANT CRAB: Oh, no. Oh, I'm suddenly very...very...sleepy. *(Giant Crab falls asleep, slipping back into the water and disappearing.)*

SUMAC: Get out of here, and don't come back. *(Picking up the flask)* A talking sparrow. A magic feather. And a giant crab. What happens next? Wait a minute, I don't want to know. I just want to get the water and get out of here. *(She approaches the water, which boils up even more violently than before. Sumac backs up and falls over backwards. The feather falls from her hand. She cowers as the Dragon emerges from the water.)*

DRAGON: Who dares to disturb the Magic Lake?

SUMAC: My name is Sumac. I came to get some water from the Magic Lake to save the life of The Inca's Son.

DRAGON: Taking water from the Magic Lake is forbidden.

SUMAC: But it's such a big lake, and I only want a tiny bit.

DRAGON: Never.

SUMAC: Please.

DRAGON: Please? Did you say, "please" to a dragon?

SUMAC: Yes.

DRAGON: That's funny. That's really funny. *(Dragon roars with laughter, then stops suddenly and cries out in pain.)*

SUMAC: What's wrong?

DRAGON: Nothing. And now, it is time for you to die.

SUMAC: My feather. It will save me. Where is it? *(She starts for the feather.)*

DRAGON: *(Stepping on the feather)* Looking for something?

SUMAC: Now that you mention it—

DRAGON: *(Lifting its foot showing the feather to her)* Is that it?

SUMAC: Oh, yes. So it is. Thank you for finding it for me.

DRAGON: Thank you? Did you say, "thank you" to a dragon? That's really funny. That's almost as funny as saying "please." "Please" and "thank you." *(Dragon roars with laughter, then stops abruptly again, crying out in pain.)*

SUMAC: Are you sure there's nothing wrong?

DRAGON: Positively. Now tell me truthfully, why do you want this feather? It wouldn't be a magic feather would it?

SUMAC: No. No. Don't be silly.

DRAGON: Are you lying to me?

SUMAC: Never.

DRAGON: You are. And because of that, you must die. Had you told me the truth, I could never have harmed you. For over the pure at heart, I have no power.

SUMAC: That's not fair. My life is in danger.

DRAGON: It doesn't matter. Because—

SUMAC: Because?

DRAGON: Because it's lunch time. *(Dragon grabs Sumac.)*

SUMAC: No. Wait. *(Just as Dragon is about to devour Sumac, it cries out in pain and releases her.)*

DRAGON: Ouch. Ouch. Ow. Ow. Darn. Ow. Ouch. Oh boy that hurts.

SUMAC: What's wrong?

DRAGON: Nothing's wrong.

SUMAC: Something has to be wrong.

DRAGON: It's just this dumb clam shell stuck in my scales.

SUMAC: So why don't you pull it out?

DRAGON: Because I can't reach it, that's why. *(Sumac approaches Dragon.)* What are you doing?

SUMAC: I'm going to pull the clam shell out.

DRAGON: You keep away from me.

SUMAC: Do you want that shell out or not?

DRAGON: You're going to hurt me. I know it.

SUMAC: I'm not going to hurt you.

DRAGON: You are.

SUMAC: Quit being such a big baby. *(She moves nearer.)*

DRAGON: *(Backing up)* No.

SUMAC: I'm not going to hurt you. *(She goes up to Dragon, who cowers and shuts his eyes. She quickly pulls out the clam shell.)*

DRAGON: *(After the clam shell is already out)* Be gentle. Please. I bruise easily. Ow. Ow. You're hurting me. You're hurting me. Ow. Ow. *(Stops; opens eyes)* Ow?

SUMAC: *(Holding up the shell)* It's out.

DRAGON: It is? It is! Wow! Yeah! Hurrah! *(Stops suddenly)* I knew that. I knew it was out. I was just pretending it hurt.

SUMAC: Of course.

DRAGON: Do you believe me?

SUMAC: I will believe whatever you want me to believe.

DRAGON: In that case, here. *(He lifts his foot so she can get the feather.)* Now hold it up towards me and shut your eyes. And when you open them, I'll be fast asleep.

SUMAC: But why?

DRAGON: Because you lied to me, I can't let you have the water. But since you helped me out, I can't kill you either. So if you use the feather to put me to sleep, I won't have to worry about doing either.

(She does as she has been told and Dragon exits.)

SCENE SEVEN

SUMAC: *(To the audience)* And so, Sumac filled the flask with water, and taking the feather in her hand, shut her eyes and wished she was at the palace of the king.

THE INCA: *(Entering with Councilor and Court Doctor)* Where did you come from?

COURT DOCTOR: She has the golden flask!

SUMAC: *(Handing the flask to The Inca)* And it's full of water.

THE INCA: *(Shaking the flask)* It is. And since the flask knows what is false and what is true, then this must be the water from the Magic Lake. Court Doctor, take it to my son.

COURT DOCTOR: Yes, Your Majesty. *(He exits)*

THE INCA: You have saved the life of my son, Sumac. What will you have as your reward?

SUMAC: The life of my brother is the only reward I want.

THE INCA: Yes, yes, yes. Your brother's miserable, little life will be spared.

(Sumac's Brother enters.)

THE INCA: *(To Sumac's Brother)* You are free to go.

SUMAC'S BROTHER: Thank you, Your Majesty.

THE INCA: *(To Sumac)* But you deserve more of a reward then this. Is there nothing else you want?

SUMAC'S BROTHER: Ask him for a pile of gold, or at least some jewels.

SUMAC: Well, there are two other things I would like.

SUMAC'S BROTHER: That's it. We're going to be rich, rich, rich!

THE INCA: What would you like?

SUMAC: I would like you to give my father and mother a larger farm.

SUMAC'S BROTHER: What do you want that for?

SUMAC: Father has been a farmer all his life. He would be unhappy if he could no longer work in the fields.

SUMAC'S BROTHER: But what about me? I hate farming. It makes my hands dirty.

THE INCA: And what is your second request?

SUMAC: My second request is that this feather be returned to the sparrow who gave it to me.

SPARROW: *(Entering)* Done. But why didn't you try to keep it for yourself? It could have made you rich beyond your wildest dreams.

SUMAC: Because it has done everything you promised me it would do. And now I have no further need of it. You trusted me with it, and now I return it to you with my thanks.
(Sparrow takes the feather and exits.)

SUMAC'S BROTHER: You are unbelievably stupid. You didn't even get anything for yourself.

THE INCA: Your brother is right. You have asked for nothing for yourself.

SUMAC: But if my brother is alive and my parents are happy, isn't that good for me as well? I may not have asked for anything for myself, but still I think I have gotten a great deal.

THE INCA: *(To Sumac's Brother)* Well?

SUMAC'S BROTHER: Well, I guess she's right. After all, I am alive. Thank you, Sumac.

SUMAC: *(To audience)* And so, the king's son drank water from the golden flask and grew up big and strong. And to sum it all up as neatly as possible—

SUMAC/THE INCA/SUMAC'S BROTHER: They all lived happily ever—

FIRE SPIRIT: *(Entering and interrupting)* Wait! What about your promise?

SUMAC: What promise?

FIRE SPIRIT: He promised me his life if his son was saved.

THE INCA: And I am ready to keep my promise.

SUMAC: You have to die?

THE INCA: Yes.

SUMAC: Right now?

THE INCA: Yes.

SUMAC: No. Absolutely, positively not.

FIRE SPIRIT: It is what has been promised. One life has been saved; another must be given.

SUMAC: Then if someone must die, take me instead. *(She leaps towards Fire Spirit.)*

SUMAC'S BROTHER: Sumac!

THE INCA: No! Stop!

(There is a great conflagration as Sumac leaps into Fire Spirit's arms.)
[SONG: THE MAGIC LAKE REPRISE begins]

SUMAC'S BROTHER: Sumac. What's happening to you?

SUMAC: I don't know. *(Sumac emerges from the fire transformed into a star.)* A great light is burning inside me. I have been transformed into a star.

SONG: MAGIC LAKE REPRISE
ENSEMBLE: *(Sings)*

Magic, Lake,
Chic-a-chic, Lake.
Magic, Lake,
Chic-a-chic, Lake.

NARRATOR: *(Speaks)* Sumac became the star of the Magic Lake.

ENSEMBLE:
(Sings under narration)

Magic, Lake,
Chic-a-chic, Lake.
Magic, Lake,
Chic-a-chic, Lake.

Star, Star, Star.
Silver star, star.

NARRATOR: *(Speaks)* And she shone high above the Magic Lake.

ENSEMBLE:
(Sings under narration)

Star, Star, Star.
Silver star, Star.

ENSEMBLE: *(Sings)*

Magic, Lake,
Chic-a-chic, Lake.
Magic, Lake,
Chic-a-chic, Lake.

Hope, Hope, Hope.
Shining hope, Hope.

NARRATOR: *(Speaks)* This star is a sign of hope for the pure at heart, high up above the Magic Lake.

ENSEMBLE:
(Sings under narration)

Hope, hope, Hope.
Shining hope, Hope.

Magic, Lake,
Chic-a-chic, Lake.
(repeat 5 times)

Magic, Lake,
Magic, Lake,
Magic! Lake!

(Singing fades out as performers exit.)

END OF PLAY

PLAYWRIGHT: David F. Eliet (script and lyrics) is a playwright director and theatre educator. As a playwright he has received many awards and grants for his writing, including a Rhode Island State Council on the Arts Playwriting Fellowship, an Alden B. Dow Creativity Fellowship, a Kennedy Center New Visions/New Voices Award. He was the winner for the Americas of the BBC International Radio Drama Contest award, among others. His scripts have been produced throughout the United States and abroad, including the BBC World Service, Frankfurt Radio in Germany, and at the Little Globe Theatre in the Ukraine. Anchorage publishes his plays *Anne and the Tiger Raja* and *The Gifts of Obidiah Oak* (both with composer Nancy Rosenberg), *The Oldest Story Ever Told*, and *Seagirl* (written under the pen name Francis Elitzig).

COMPOSER: Nancy Rosenberg (music) received her A.B. in Music and Comparative Literature from Brown University, and holds a M.A. in Musicology from Boston University. Her career encompasses a wide range of musical pursuits. A prolific composer of music for theatre, her credits include five full-length musicals and many musical plays for children, including the 1993 winner of the New Visions/New Voices award:*The Sun's Musicians*, written in collaboration with David F. Eliet. She has worked as a composer, sound designer, and arranger on numerous commercial projects for children, among them a recent book/CD set for *Kindermusik,* and various best-selling children's software titles such as *The Three Grouchketeers*, *Elmo Through the Looking Glass*, *Sesame Street Music Maker*, and *Elmo's Adventures in Grouchland*. In addition to her work as a composer, Ms. Rosenberg is active as a musical director, vocalist, and teacher. Specializing in jazz and popular vocal styles, she currently serves on the faculty of Brown University's Applied Music Program while pursuing a doctorate in Music Education at Boston University.